Brain Smart
Strategies
for Helping Your
Anxious Child

Patricia Pantelias Gage, PhD

Library of Congress Control Number: 2021900845

Softcover ISBN 978-1-7357393-3-5

Cover design by Aaron Welch
Big A Marketing
www.bigamarketing.com

Printed in the United States
First Edition, March 2021
www.BrainSmartAcademics.com

Dedication

This book is dedicated to school psychologists who have devoted their lives' work to enhancing the mental health and educational competence of children. They do more than simply test children. They have unique expertise in mental health, learning, and behavior to help all the children in our schools reach their potential academically, socially, and behaviorally.

Acknowledgment

I gratefully acknowledge my extraordinary editor, Tracy Hundley, for her expertise, attention to detail, and enormous patience in enriching and organizing the manuscript.

Contents

PART
ONE

Introduction

Your child throws up before getting on the school bus every morning. He cries uncontrollably, begging you to let him stay home instead of going to school. He is certain that today his math teacher will call on him to work on a problem on the board in front of the class, and that he won't remember how to do it and everyone will laugh at him. You make a point to wake him up in a positive and loving way each day, but he refuses to get out of bed, complaining of a severe stomachache, a headache, a sore throat...and the list goes on. He puts the covers over his head and tells you to go away and let him sleep. You try to calmly reassure him that everything is going to be okay, but nothing helps. You offer to drive him to school as a special treat, and he finally agrees, but when you arrive, he refuses to get out of the car as he screams and cries, holding up the line of cars behind you waiting to pull in and drop off.

Take heart. Your child is not behaving this way because he is spoiled, is stubborn, or simply being oppositional. Your child needs help. What you are experiencing and observing are common signs of an anxiety disorder.

Some anxiety is a normal human emotion and certainly common. However, one in 8 children under the age of 18 suffers from excessive worry and anxiety, which affects school performance and daily interactions and can lead to substance abuse and depression. Of children 3 to 17 years of age, 7% have a diagnosed anxiety disorder at any given time, and nearly 1 out of every 3 adolescents meets the criteria for an anxiety disorder by the age of 18. Harvard Medical School's 2017 National Comorbidity Survey estimates that the lifetime prevalence of anxiety disorders of any kind among U.S. adolescents was 31.9%. Of those adolescents with an anxiety disorder, an estimated 8.3% had severe impairment. The prevalence of anxiety disorders among adolescents was higher for females (38.0%) than for males (26.1%). Despite the prevalence of anxiety in children, according to the Anxiety and Depression Association of America (2017), anxiety in children often goes undiagnosed and untreated. Anxiety disorders often persist over time and do not go away on their own. When left untreated, anxiety takes a toll on a child's daily life and can lead to depression.

As a licensed school psychologist who has worked in both schools and private practice for more than 30 years, I believe my most gratifying and memorable experiences of working with anxious children are those in which I have worked in close partnership with the child's parents. When parents have a strong commitment to work with their child on a day-to-day basis, in between counseling sessions, we achieve the greatest results and the child benefits the most. Therefore, I wrote this book to make it easier for parents to remember and refer to various anxiety strategies and to coach their children to practice the strategies regularly, even after therapy ends.

Today more than ever, it is important for parents, teachers, health care professionals, and caregivers to recognize the symptoms of a child suffering from excessive worry and anxiety. When a child engages in a challenging behavior at school or at home, the behavior is often due to the demands and expectations placed on them relative to the skills in their repertoire to meet those demands. Therefore, the most effective way to address the challenging behavior is to teach the child specific coping techniques and, most importantly, to give the child ample time to learn and practice those techniques without fear of consequence or punishment. When children are reminded and encouraged to practice coping skills on a regular basis, they are more apt to use them on their own when needed. Giving children well-tested, developmentally appropriate strategies and encouraging them to express their emotions in an appropriate manner are as essential as teaching them to read and write.

This book provides parents of preteens—children ages 9 through 13—information about anxiety disorders as well as strategies for helping their anxious children and for turning difficult situations into positive experiences. Parents will learn to use the issues preteens are dealing with as teaching moments, thereby building resilience and giving their children the tools they need to face their worries and fears today and in the years to come. Parents also will learn how to regulate their own stress response to keep a tense and anxious situation from escalating, and how to avoid common pitfalls when trying to support their anxious children.

I based this book on questions my patients and their parents frequently ask, while also trying to be succinct for today's busy parents. I recommend reading Chapters 1 through 9 first to fully understand the issue of anxiety and how these well-tested strategies and interventions can help you deal with it. As you read through the questions and answers, try to keep an open mind. In my practice, both parents and children sometimes dismiss a strategy when I first suggest it. For example, when I suggest practicing deep breathing, I'm not surprised when I get incredulous laughs from some. But if they truly listen as I explain the reason behind breathing exercises, I quickly gain their full attention. So as you read, strive to be receptive to new ideas, focus on the content, and commit to consistently practicing the strategies with your child and coaching him or her with empathy.

Once you have read Part One, use Part Two on an ongoing basis as you work with your anxious child. When faced with a difficult situation, review the *Toolkit of Brain-Smart Strategies* to determine which one you want to try. As you try each strategy, document how well it worked for your child in the *Strategy Log*. As you continue to try different strategies, the log will remind you at a glance which interventions have and have not been helpful for your child in the past. Last but not least, consider expanding your understanding of anxiety even more by reading some of the additional resources listed on page 119.

CHAPTER 1
Anxiety Explained

So, what exactly is anxiety? It is more than simply a feeling. Children with anxiety disorders frequently have intense, excessive and persistent worry and fear about everyday situations. They are likely to experience intrusive thoughts and a feeling of apprehension about what is going to happen in the future. While we do not know what causes anxiety disorders, we know that several things play a significant role, such as genetics, brain chemistry, over-reactive fight, flight, or freeze responses, stressful life events, and possibly learned behavior from the environment. Anxious children tend to have an inhibited, overly cautious, and somewhat tentative temperament that predisposes them to anxiety disorders (Huberty, 2008). In school they struggle keeping up with all the demands and tend to be inattentive, perfectionistic, and often forgetful. They often refuse to participate out of excessive concerns about failure or embarrassment or just seek overly easy assignments, giving the impression of not being motivated.

According to the Diagnostic and Statistical Manual of Mental Disorders, Fifth Edition (DSM-V), which psychologists use as an authoritative guide for diagnosing mental disorders, a panic attack or anxiety attack is an abrupt surge of intense fear or intense discomfort that reaches a peak within minutes and during which time four or more of the following symptoms must occur: a feeling of imminent danger or doom, a rapid heartbeat, trembling, sweating, a choking feeling, a fear of dying, dizziness or lightheadedness, chest pain or discomfort, shortness of breath or a smothered feeling, feeling the need to escape, a feeling of losing control or "going crazy," tingling sensations, chills, or hot flushes. While the symptoms might last 10 to15 minutes, they are scary and those few minutes might feel like a lifetime to a child.

These anxiety symptoms are the body's physical fight, flight, or freeze reaction to a perceived threat. Worry is common, normal, and sometimes even helpful in keeping your children safe, such as when they're riding their bikes or learning to swim. However, under prolonged stress, worry can turn into an unhealthy amount of anxiety. It can venture into **overestimating**—magnifying the likelihood something bad will happen (e.g., your child might be overly worried that he is going to embarrass himself and everyone will laugh at him)—or **catastrophizing**—imagining the worst possible thing is about to happen (e.g., your child might think he will faint, have a heart attack, or die as a result of his panic attack). A preoccupation with "what ifs" and worst-case scenarios can become a problem that interferes with daily life.

Are there different kinds of anxiety?

The DSM-V outlines the following major types of anxiety disorders. Note that not all children fit neatly into a particular diagnostic category, however. In clinical practice, seeing a spectrum of symptoms with overlap is more likely.

Separation anxiety disorder is specific to children and frequently associated with the fear of leaving familiar people—parents, caregivers, or other people they are attached to. Some separation anxiety is generally considered a normal part of early child development, but when it becomes excessive, it can negatively impact a child's development. Children suffering from separation anxiety worry that something bad will happen to them if they separate from their parents or caregivers. They often refuse to leave their homes, do not want to go to sleepovers, do not want to attend school (referred to as "school refusal"), ask to sleep with their parents because they are afraid to sleep alone, and generally appear overly clingy. Persistent separation anxiety might indicate excessive worry about family matters, safety issues, or being rejected.

Phobias are intense, specific, extreme, and irrational fears that last at least six months. This might be a fear of animals, objects, or situations. A toddler's typical fear of the dark or of sitting on the "potty" is not considered a phobia. A common phobia is **agoraphobia**, a fear of entering open or large crowded places or of being in places from which it might be difficult to escape. A person with agoraphobia usually feels trapped and has intense feelings of helplessness, which often causes panic and embarrassment. Another common phobia is **claustrophobia**, the extreme or irrational fear of confined spaces.

Social anxiety disorder (also known as **social phobia**) is the fear of being rejected, embarrassed, or negatively judged in a social setting. This is particularly prevalent among preteens since they tend to worry about embarrassing themselves in front of their peers and are afraid of saying the wrong thing or being evaluated negatively by others, such as coaches and teachers. When this developmentally normal type of worry slips into social phobia, preteens begin worrying excessively and are likely to avoid social gatherings, sports, and group activities, significantly compromising their lifestyles and learning experiences. Though they avoid interacting with others, some of these children still might feel comfortable with some close friends and family.

Selective mutism is a disorder often observed in children who have social phobia and are dealing with social anxiety. Children with selective mutism cannot speak when anxiety is triggered by specific social situations or by specific people, even though they have the ability to both speak and understand language. For example, one of my former patients was a first-grader who spoke at home (as evidenced by the home videos her parents showed me) but would not talk to anyone in her school other than her teacher—and she would speak to her teacher only in the classroom closet. She initially agreed to participate in sessions with me in that same closet, and I felt very special when she eventually agreed to meet in my office. Giving her a little control allowed me to build rapport and much needed trust.

Selective mutism is often used by young children as an avoidance strategy to reduce their distress in social situations. Their consistent failure to speak causes them to avoid certain social situations and can be quite debilitating. Some additional findings with this group of children are difficulty maintaining eye contact, blank expressions with some reluctance to smile, difficulty expressing feelings, and sensitivity to crowds and noise.

Panic disorder causes panic attacks, which are the physical sensations of the brain's alarm system: a racing heart, rapid breathing, sweating, and trembling at inappropriate times, when no danger is present. Panic attacks can be triggered by something specific or occur out of the blue. They usually reach their peak within 15 minutes. Children with panic disorder begin to avoid situations they think will cause a panic attack, and they experience ongoing worry that they will have another attack. Because of the unexpected and unpleasant sensations of panic attacks, children believe they have serious medical problems, which lands them in doctors' offices too frequently. They might go through mega work-ups to rule out endocrine, cardiac, and neurological causes of their symptoms. Even after they are reassured that nothing is medically wrong with them, the fear of panic attacks often becomes the cause of panic attacks, creating a vicious circle. However, never tell a child with panic disorder that it's "all in his head." Not only is this statement unhelpful, it can cause the child even more distress.

Generalized anxiety disorder is defined by persistent and excessive worry about many things, like the possibility of a natural disaster, school performance, relationships with friends, and so on. The worry of a child with generalized anxiety disorder is so intense that it affects the child's concentration, makes him very irritable most of the time, causes muscle tension in different parts of the body, and produces other physical symptoms discussed in more detail in *Chapter 3: Fight, Flight, or Freeze.*

There are two disorders that used to be grouped with anxiety disorders but are now classified under their own separate categories because they have unique causes and require unique treatments. However, they are so closely related to anxiety disorders that knowing about them is helpful. **Obsessive-compulsive disorder** is characterized by the compulsion to do something repetitively, such as hand washing, and often involves excessive orderliness, ritualistic behavior, and a need for control. **Post traumatic stress disorder** is triggered by a terrifying event and involves flashbacks, nightmares, and feeling frightened when not in danger.

How is worry different from anxiety?

While anxiety and worry are often used interchangeably, anxiety is not the same as worry. Worry is what happens when your mind dwells on negative thoughts, uncertain outcomes, or things that might go wrong. Worrying is usually focused on the future, on what might happen. Worry is strictly cognitive (mental), whereas anxiety has both a cognitive element and a physiological response. In other words, worry happens only in the mind while anxiety is experienced with both mind and body. In fact, worry is often referred to as the cognitive construct of anxiety.

How can I tell whether my child is experiencing normal worry versus excessive worry and anxiety?

The primary characteristic of anxiety is excessive worry, which is fear that some new or future event will have a negative outcome for oneself or a loved one. Signs of anxiety differ between the anxious and non-anxious child mostly in degree, persistence, and variety of symptoms. An anxious child is much more likely than his peers to interpret minor issues or events as potentially threatening or dangerous. For example, an assignment to give a brief oral report in class typically leaves most children feeling a bit concerned about their performance, but an anxious child is likely to worry that his report will be a total disaster and a complete embarrassment. See *Determining When Anxiety Is a Problem* on page 74 for a list of signs that your child is struggling with anxiety and probably needs intervention.

How direct should I be with my child about his anxiety?

For children to manage anxiety, they need to understand what is happening inside their minds and bodies. They need to know that the feelings they are experiencing have physiological causes. This knowledge can lessen the symptoms of anxiety (Chansky, 2014, Wilson & Lyons, 2013) and, along with coping skills, allow them to process and move through anxious states successfully. Therefore, talking to your child about her anxiety, helping her to recognize it, and encouraging her to open up about her fears and worries is important. However, go slowly; do not overwhelm her with too much information at once.

You can start a dialogue about anxiety with your child by explaining that it runs in families, which might be the reason your child is experiencing anxiety. When a parent is diagnosed with an anxiety disorder, his or her child is 7 times more likely to develop anxiety (Ginsberg, Drake, Tein, Teetsel & Riddle, 2015; Wilson & Lyons, 2013). Also noteworthy, 65% of children living with an anxious parent meet the criteria for an anxiety disorder (Ginsburg, et al., 2015).

Also be sure to explain to your child that even if there is no family history of anxiety, a person can develop anxiety after something terrible happens, like having an accident or going through a significant change due to a major illness, the loss of a loved one, a move to a different state, or a divorce. You can discuss whether something like this in your child's life might have triggered anxiety and share some of your own experiences with traumatic events.

Encourage conversation by sharing some things you were overly scared about when you were her age, and ask her if she has ever had a similar fear or worry. As a means to generate discussion, describe a recent situation in which you observed her exhibiting signs of extreme anxiety. As your child shares her worries and fears, remember to always offer reassurance that having these feelings is okay. As you talk, make every effort to remain calm because studies clearly indicate that emotions are contagious, especially from people we spend a lot of time with.

Point out that anxiety might feel uncomfortable, but it doesn't last long; it is temporary and it is certainly not dangerous. Most importantly, it is treatable. Anxiety is usually uncomplicated, fairly redundant, and often exaggerated because of the excessive need for certainty about what is going to happen, how long something uncomfortable is going to last, and what the outcome will be.

Explaining to children that the emotions they are experiencing have physiological causes is a key component to successful treatment. Children are more likely to try coping strategies when they understand the way their brains function. (See *Chapter 3: Fight, Flight, or Freeze* on page 23 for more detail.) When they understand the physical symptoms of anxiety—a change in breathing, uneasiness in the stomach, tightness in the chest—they can more easily recognize the onset of anxiety, determine whether a real threat exists, and implement strategies to return to a calm state.

CHAPTER 2
The Challenging Preteen Years

While anxiety affects people of all ages, this book focuses on helping parents of preteens, children ages 9 through 13.

Why focus on the preteen years?

The preteen developmental stages are ripe for anxiety. Children this age are moving toward independence and are in the process of developing decision-making skills. They are starting to consider what they might want to do in the future as they shift their attention from play-centered interests to academics. This shift places more pressure than normal on performing in school and competing with the same-aged peers.

In the preteen phase of development, children look to peers and media for information and advice, with friends greatly influencing their decisions. They develop greater capability for social conscience, and they become more capable of abstract thought, understanding complicated issues, and taking on more responsibility in their homes.

Preteens tend to want to blend in with, rather than stand out from, their peers, and they tend to get overly concerned about outward appearance; they don't want to be different from their peers in any way. They tend to be self-conscious and self-centered. They care a great deal about their relationships with peers, often giving peers greater importance than family.

Preteens often experience a significant drop in self-esteem and overall confidence to try new things and tackle difficult learning tasks. After all, if they do not try something, they will not look like a failure or feel incapable.

Preteens seek privacy, spending a lot of time in their bedrooms. They often go to great lengths to separate from and appear independent from their families. Their way of exerting their independence can at times leave parents highly drained of energy.

Preteens are capable of thinking logically, but the developing prefrontal cortex (the part of the brain responsible for planning, decision-making, problem-solving, and self-control) is still immature. This can negatively affect focus and impulse control.

All of these things—more pressure to perform in school, the struggle for acceptance from peers, the drop in self-esteem, increased time spent alone, and difficulty focusing and controlling impulses—can serve as triggers to excessive worrying and anxiety. Therefore, the preteen years are a very important time to learn and practice strategies for handling anxiety.

Are there specific situations anxious kids should avoid?

A child may be anxious for numerous reasons. However, instead of focusing on the "why" and what situations to avoid, focusing on providing the child with coping skills is much more helpful. Life is not easy for an anxious child, and while he might be able to avoid a known anxiety-producing situation, a new triggering situation might arise at any time. However, good coping skills can be applied to all possible triggers of anxiety.

That said, being mindful of some common anxiety-triggering life events is valuable. If you know a situation might cause your anxious preteen more anxiety than usual, you can prepare him for it. For example, "Bob invited 10 children to his birthday party. That many kids talking and having fun will be a little noisy." If you want your child to do something new, describe exactly what he should do and what to expect. For example, "When you go to the counter to order ice cream by yourself, the cashier will expect you to tell her what flavor and size you want and whether you want it in a bowl or cone. Then she will ask you to pay for it, give you change, and leave to get your ice cream. You can stand nearby and wait for her to give it to you." Encourage him and be available for support as he first tries it. "You can do it. I'll be close by."

The goal is for your child to gradually learn to reduce avoidance and push through the discomfort that comes with anxiety. See *Preparing Your Child for New Experiences* on page 81 for a list of frequent anxiety-inducing stressors.

Are some children more susceptible to anxiety?

While all preteens are susceptible to anxiety, early exposure to chronic sources of stress is particularly debilitating and should be taken into account in treatment. Chronic stress significantly affects children's developing brains and their overall emotional wellness. Preteens who have suffered neglect, loss, abuse, bullying, family addiction, mental illness, unrealistic expectations, frequent moves, scary or traumatic events, or a decrease of communication among family members from an early age need your help the most.

CHAPTER 3
Fight, Flight, or Freeze

Some worry and anxiety is normal. The brain has a full-time alarm system that is constantly on the lookout for potential threats. When it identifies overwhelming threats or fearful events, the brain triggers a fight, flight, or freeze response. This response is helpful when truly in danger, but when this response occurs repeatedly when no real danger is present, anxiety develops.

What is the fight, flight, or freeze response?

Have you ever noticed that when you are worrying and your mind is full of "what ifs," your body responds? You might experience a racing heart, rapid breathing, perspiration, sweaty palms, tingling in the hands, or butterflies in the stomach. This is the fight, flight, or freeze response, the body's reaction to fear, and it serves a purpose in responding to danger (Chansky, 2014, Wilson & Lyons, 2013). People have experienced the fight, flight, or freeze response since the beginning of time. Imagine you are a cavewoman and you come face to face with a hungry, fearsome tiger. You can pick up a big stick and try to injure, kill, or scare the tiger away (fight), you can run from the tiger (flight), or you can stand very still and let the tiger eat you (freeze). Obviously, that last one is not a good choice! But usually, when people cannot fight or run, they shut down and freeze.

The fight, flight, or freeze response is an unconscious response; it is triggered automatically. The brain's prefrontal cortex continuously scans for danger. When it detects a threat, it sends a signal to the brain's amygdala. Then the body goes on autopilot and does a number of things to get ready for action. Stress hormones such as adrenaline and cortisol are released. The heart rate increases, which helps pump more blood to the muscles and brain, which in turn causes increased alertness, sharper focus, and extra energy. The lungs take in air more quickly, supplying the body with more oxygen. The digestive system slows. The pupils enlarge, increasing the sharpness of vision. While all of this is happening, physical, often unpleasant, sensations are experienced in the body—tightness in the chest, bellyaches, dizziness, a feeling that something bad is going to happen. This is the feeling of anxiety.

What exactly is the prefrontal cortex and amygdala?

Essentially two parts of the brain are involved in anxiety: the prefrontal cortex and the amygdala. The prefrontal cortex is the part of the brain that helps you come up with rational, logical responses. It makes sure you process information analytically, use good judgment, consider the consequences of actions and decisions, plan ahead before doing something, and concentrate better. It is where rational thought takes place. The prefrontal cortex is responsible for taking in data through the body's senses, analyzing the data, and then deciding what actions to take. If it decides that something is a threat or dangerous, it sends a message to the amygdala.

The amygdala is a tiny, almond-shaped cluster of nuclei located deep in the lower part of the brain called the limbic system, the part of the brain that deals with emotions and mood. The amygdala is responsible for recognizing danger and preparing the body to react. Sometimes the amygdala is triggered because of a "potential danger" message received from the prefrontal cortex, and sometimes the amygdala is triggered directly from sensory input. Either way, the amygdala essentially functions as the body's panic button or, as some call it, the alarm system. It is designed to send a signal when there is danger present, but it is unable to differentiate between real and perceived danger. When the amygdala senses any fear or notices any potential danger, it sends signals to the hypothalamus (the part of the brain that, among other things, regulates emotional responses), which triggers a fight, flight, or freeze response. In other words, it puts the body into survival mode. So while the prefrontal cortex can initiate a fear response, the amygdala is what produces excessive fear and ultimately the anxiety response.

The prefrontal cortex and the amygdala are supposed to work together to help you in times of danger. However, sometimes the amygdala activates for every worrisome thought that enters the brain. These "false alarms" can be quite problematic.

Why do false alarms happen?

False alarms occur for multiple reasons. They might occur because chemicals in the brain's nerve cells are out of balance and thus not working the way they are supposed to. In people with increased cortisol levels, the amygdala sends alarms way too often, when no real danger exists. Their faulty alarm systems can be triggered by all kinds of things: loud noises, crowds, smells, perceived slights, dentist visits, airplanes, and so on. When the fight, flight, or freeze response keeps getting activated, the alarm switch eventually gets stuck in the ON position. This results in being hypersensitive, on high alert for trivial stressors on a daily basis.

False alarms also occur because in the anxious brain, the amygdala is large and hypersensitive. It sends false alarms often because the amygdala is sensing threats even in non-threatening situations. Thus, children with anxiety disorders tend to feel threatened more often than children without anxiety disorders.

Prolonged anxiety also weakens the connection between the amygdala and the prefrontal cortex. Therefore, in anxious people, when the amygdala alerts the brain to danger, the prefrontal cortex does not kick in as expected to help them come up with rational, logical responses. Instead full-blown panic ensues, regardless of the nature of the threat.

What is the best way to explain fight, flight, or freeze to preteens?

Using the analogy of a smoke alarm is an effective way to explain the fight, flight, or freeze response to preteens. The discussion can go something like this:

"You have smoke alarms in your house to alert you if there is a fire. But sometimes, a smoke alarm is too sensitive. It might go off when a little sauce spills in the oven, or when you burn your toast—when there's no real fire. If the smoke alarm keeps going off for no good reason, constantly jarring you and interfering with your day, you will want to fix it.

"The part of the brain called the amygdala is like your smoke alarm; it alerts you when there is danger, like when a school bully is after you or when you climb something very tall and get too close to the edge. It creates a feeling of anxiety that helps you escape the danger. But if the amygdala is too sensitive, and keeps going off when no real danger is present (for example, when something simply feels dangerous, like taking a test or giving a presentation in front of the class), then you will feel anxious, jittery, uncomfortable, and physically ill much of the time. These feelings can be scary. They make it hard to think clearly and concentrate on your work. You might feel so overwhelmed that you stop doing things or going places to avoid feeling bad. This is when using brain-smart strategies can help."

Once your child understands what is happening in her body when she feels anxious, she might wonder why she has so many false alarms when many of her peers do not seem to. You can explain that false alarms are caused by stressors—situations perceived as a threat to one's safety and emotional well-being—and that everyone's perception is different. What one person perceives as a threat others may not. You can also explain that brain chemistry, past experiences, personality, age, and varying sensitivities all contribute to one's perception of threats.

As a parent, how do I respond to a false alarm situation?

When your child is reacting to a false alarm, you can say things like "stop thinking about it" or "don't worry" or "it's not as bad as you think" until you turn blue in the face, but it will not help. Every false alarm weakens the part of the brain that allows logical thinking, eventually shutting it down altogether, leaving your child in a highly emotional state. When in this state, your child cannot stop her reaction and cannot even truly listen to what you are saying. Her response to the false alarm is the same as if a tiger or bear were about to attack her. She disconnects from her "thinking" brain (what scientists call the smart brain), and her "protector brain" (what scientists call the worry brain) takes over with only one goal: to move away from what is happening to safety.

Instead of trying to reason with your child about the situation or lecture her at that moment, reassure her that you are there for her, acknowledge her emotions, help label her feelings, and help her to calm down until she learns to do it on her own automatically.

CHAPTER 4
The Worry Wheel

One of my patients who suffered from anxiety was a somaticizer, a person who experiences anxiety mostly through body sensations (Chansky, 2014), so he often feared that he was critically sick. Because of the constant physical symptoms, he repeatedly asked his parents to take him to doctors to be reassured. He was not able to tell his parents or me what was worrying him, but he could list his physical symptoms, such as headaches, stomachaches, and heart palpitations. Once, during a therapy session, he described his experience as being on a "worry wheel." He explained that the worry wheel kept speeding up and making him sick. His expression was so poignant that I use it in my practice to this day.

What is the worry wheel?

The child who coined the phrase suffered from challenges to both his emotional and physical health due to excessive worrying. He was always on high alert, overly sensitive to any signs of uncertainty or risk in his daily life. He felt like he was on a worry wheel because he was constantly going to doctors for check-ups and tests to figure out what was wrong with him, which he really disliked, but he kept feeling so bad that he could not stop worrying that he was seriously ill, and that if he didn't get checked, he was going to die. Every physical discomfort he experienced, such as headaches or nausea, set the wheel in motion, and his life became consumed with going back and forth to the hospital for tests and unpleasant doctor visits. His parents often called me to say, "He's back on the worry wheel and his negative self-talk is out of control," and, "his physical symptoms are multiplying by the minute."

Why is my child on the worry wheel?

Anxiety can lie dormant in children's minds until an incident brings their concerns about their health to the forefront, setting the worry wheel in motion. As children experience physical symptoms and exaggerated concerns about their health, they experience panicky feelings that often lead to doctor visits in search of reassurance. This constant checking and possible testing can lead to a tendency toward isolation from others, sending these children around the worry wheel once again and even getting them into a depressed state.

What does it feel like to be on the worry wheel?

Children with anxiety report worrying non-stop for hours. They feel tense and restless but do not know why or have any idea how to stop it. They try to avoid thinking about the negative and often catastrophic thoughts constantly running through their heads, but they simply cannot. They report feeling tired, being unable to focus or sleep, and lacking the interest or energy to get things done.

Getting my child off the worry wheel poses a challenge. How can I help my child?

The good news is that these states of anxiety and worry respond well to children confronting and challenging their underlying fears, thereby exposing them as unrealistic and false. The worry wheel represents a process in their thinking and in their bodily sensations. The best way to help children get off the wheel is to calm them physically using the relaxation strategies described in *Chapter 5: Relax!*

When my former patient began fretting and worrying, his parents helped him by reminding him that he was on the worry wheel. That was his cue to do deep breathing exercises so he could gain control and get off the worry wheel before he became too ill.

When your child is in full swing on the worry wheel, do not tell her things like, "Stop worrying," or, "Don't be scared." Instead, empathize and validate her feelings. Encourage her to put her feelings and fears into words rather than denying the validity of her feelings. Remind her to practice some of the strategies that have worked for her before or suggest she try a new strategy. Showing her that you understand how she might be feeling and that you believe in her offers more comfort and is more likely to help her jump off the worry wheel.

CHAPTER 5
Relax!

A critical tool for combating anxiety is the ability to intentionally relax, even in stressful situations. This is not easy, especially for young children who are maturing and still learning how to recognize and deal with stress.

How can I help my child learn to relax?

Some relaxation techniques include breathing exercises, distraction, imagery and visualization, progressive muscle relaxation, activities involving repetitive movement, and the use of scents. The best way to coach your child through these relaxation techniques is by practicing them together with him on an ongoing basis. To ensure success, practice these relaxation techniques consistently. By doing so, you build a closer relationship with your child, reap the benefits of the exercises yourself, and increase your ability to maintain a calm, firm, and consistent manner. Remember that your child will need repetitive practice and occasional reminders on how to self-calm and cool down. And be prepared for skepticism. When preteens are asked to do deep belly breathing exercises, the usual response is, "I already know how to breathe!" It is important they understand the purpose of breathing exercises because if they think the exercises are useless, they are not likely to do them. Explain to your child why they work and encourage him to at least try them!

Why DO breathing exercises help?

The breath typically is shallow and rapid during an anxiety attack and deeper and slower during times of relaxation. The purpose of a breathing exercise is to focus on your breath, use your diaphragm to breathe, and intentionally change your breathing pattern. When you inhale deeply, the diaphragm expands, placing pressure on the organs in the abdomen, which activates the vagus nerve, a cranial nerve that runs from the brain to the abdomen. The vagus nerve then sends a signal through the spine to the brain, activating the relaxation response. The brain then quickly reduces stress response symptoms like a fast heart rate, jittery feelings, and foggy thinking. When you force the breath into a relaxed state, the mind follows. See *Doing Belly Breathing Exercises* on page 101 for instructions on breathing exercises.

A parent recently shared with me that her sixth-grade daughter was worrying excessively about an oral class presentation. She worried before, during, and after the presentation, saying, "Mom, what if everyone laughs at me?" "What if my mind goes totally blank and I can't remember a word of what I'm supposed to say?" "What if I get a bad grade and fail the class?" Once the presentation was over, instead of feeling relieved, she continued to worry, expressing regrets of what she could have and should have said or done during the presentation instead. I recommended they try a yoga class together at their local YMCA. The instructor taught them how to take deep belly breaths using the diaphragm. She told them to practice this deep breathing the minute "what ifs" start to flood their thoughts. They found the exercises to be a lot of fun. They now practice deep breathing together twice a day, even if they are not worried about anything. For about 10 minutes, they pay close attention to how their breath feels without thinking about anything else. They enjoy the special time together and report that switching to deep breathing when something stressful happens has become second nature. Getting to this point was a gradual process and took a lot of encouragement to stay with the classes, but it was well worth it for both of them.

How can distraction help my child relax?

Sometimes doing deep, slow breathing is not enough to distract the brain from all the "what ifs" bombarding it, or the environment is not conducive to focusing on deep breathing. When needed, your child can distract himself from his current worries by giving himself a time-out of sorts. For example, if in a chaotic or loud environment, he might move to a quiet corner and count backward from 30 to 1. If in a classroom, he might excuse himself to go to the restroom to calm down. Before taking a big test or doing a presentation, the sixth-grader I mentioned previously learned to ask her teacher for permission to go to the restroom, where she splashes her face with cold water and does her counting and deep breathing until she is calm enough to return to the classroom. This strategy works well for her. See *Using Distractions* on page 96 for a list of ideas.

My child tends to be more of a visual learner. What kind of imagery and visualization will help my child relax?

When your child feels anxious and overwhelmed, you might encourage her to shut her eyes for a few moments and imagine her "happy place"—a place, situation, or activity that she associates with being happy and calm. This technique described in *Using Visualization and Guided Imagery* on page 100 often helps children to relax themselves and get into a state of calm.

Everyone has a different happy place. One of my patients described his as lying on a sandy beach his family used to visit on holidays, listening to the surf come in and out. His active and energetic brother's happy place, on the other hand, was scaling a climbing wall and reaching the very top all by himself. What works for one child might not work for another. (See the last page of this book for photos of my happy place!)

Helping your child determine her happy place might take some trial and error. Help her personalize her happy place by asking her to recall some of her favorite memories. Ask her what she looks forward to doing after school or on the weekends, or what she wishes she could do if there were no restrictions or limitations.

Once she has a happy place firmly in mind, coach her on visualizing being there. Encourage her to imagine as much detail as possible, for example, in my patient's case, the sound of the ocean, the smell of the salt in the air, the warmth of the sun, and the feeling of the sand molding to his body. The more vivid her imagery, the more calming it will be. Have her practice visualizing her happy place occasionally so that invoking the imagery during stressful times becomes easier.

What is progressive relaxation and how will it help my child relax?

Anxiety often leads to tight and tense muscles. Because the mind and body are so connected, activating relaxation of the body can help calm emotions as well. However, willing the entire body to relax is difficult and not usually successful. Progressive relaxation—focusing on relaxing one body part at a time—is a more attainable goal and eventually results in the entire body being relaxed.

This approach helps children learn and understand how their bodies feel when they are worried. It allows them to recognize tension in their bodies, such as tight muscles, faster heartbeats, uneasiness in the stomach, and so on.

Specific instructions on progressive relaxation are in *Doing Progressive Relaxation Exercises* on page 102. Start by leading your child through the steps, with the ultimate goal of your child learning to lead himself through progressive relaxation. As you practice, remind your child to pay close attention to each muscle group, noticing the difference between tense muscles and relaxed muscles. Encourage him to let go of each body part until his whole body relaxes and goes limp. Sometimes kids can get silly doing this, and it can be a lot of fun. You can do it with them as well.

How do activities involving repetitive movement help my child relax?

When your child is experiencing anxiety, he is trapped in his internal world of thoughts and feelings, which builds more and more stress in his mind and body. Repetitive movement is a relaxation tool that releases unwanted energy in a physical, positive way. Such movement will help him get out of his head and become more grounded to reality. Repetitive activities can be quite physical, such as rocking and swinging, or less physical, such as clapping, tapping, or squeezing a stress ball. These activities temporarily distract preteens from their worries, which helps them relax and feel calmer. See *Engaging in Repetitive Movement* on page 97 for a list of ideas.

How can I use scents to help my child relax?

Many people report that breathing in pleasant scents, such as essential oils, is calming. Certain scents like lavender have been shown to boost mood, calm the mind, and relax the body. While scents might not have a calming effect on everyone, I generally encourage my patients to at least try it. If you find that scents help your child relax, she can use scent as an extra "bonus tool" when she does breathing or relaxation exercises, when she studies, when she is preparing for bedtime, or at any other time she is intentional about relaxing. See *Using Scent as a Relaxation Tool* on page 105 for a list of ideas.

Okay, my child has relaxed. Now what?

Once your child feels calm and relaxed, he is in a better place to talk about his worries with someone he trusts. Together you can come up with ways to deal with what is bothering him at that moment and brainstorm what he can do in that situation. Ask him how his body is feeling (e.g., headache, stomachache, rapid heart rate). Then, encourage him to label the emotion he is feeling (e.g., angry, sad, scared) and point out that everyone feels that emotion at times. Next, ask him what his thoughts about it are and what is he telling himself as a result (e.g., *They'll laugh at me*), and finally, discuss what actions he is taking as a result (e.g., school avoidance, isolation from friends). This connects the three important parts of anxiety for your child: what **physical symptoms** he is having, what **anxious thoughts** he is experiencing, and what **avoidance behaviors**, or actions, he is engaging in. He might need your help to make these connections and help identify and label his feelings until he can do it on his own. You want your child to realize that anxiety and **not any real danger** is causing him to miss out on opportunities and fun events in his life.

As you engage him in this manner, he will be more able to identify what thoughts and worries contributed to his anxious state. He will be more open to suggestions on what to do next time, such as utilizing more of these relaxation techniques, listening to music he loves, expressing his feelings verbally, or something else. This is the time to remind your child that though he might not always be able to change or control what happens to him, he can certainly control how he reacts; he can **choose how he deals with it**.

CHAPTER 6
Negative Self-Talk

A contributing factor to anxiety is negative self-talk, an inner dialogue in which one magnifies the negative aspects of a situation, minimizes the positive aspects, assumes self-blame when something goes wrong, blows things out of proportion, or sees results as black or white (success or failure), allowing no room for shades of gray.

Why is my child more often focused on the negative than on the positive?

Believe it or not, the human brain is hard-wired to focus on the negative. This helps us survive as a species, and especially helped our ancestors who regularly faced life-threatening dangers. While humans have evolved, our brains still tune in much more to the negative things we hear, see, and feel than to the positive so that we can protect ourselves from (real or imagined) danger. After all, the brain is an efficient organ; it does not alert us to positive things because we do not need to do anything to survive positive situations.

43

This propensity to focus on the negative results is what is known as the negativity bias, or the negativity effect—the theory that when one has both negative and positive experiences in equal intensity, the negative experiences have a greater effect on one's psychological state and processes than the positive or neutral experiences. For example, imagine you are on a beautiful hike, thoroughly enjoying yourself, but along the trail you trip and come very close to falling off a cliff. If you are like most people, you will remember those five seconds of thinking you might fall much more vividly than the hours of beautiful scenery you experienced during the rest of your hike.

How important are my child's inner thoughts on his emotional state?

As parents, you might think that your child's emotions and worried thoughts are caused by outside factors—events or other people. In actuality, "things" do not make your child feel emotions; your child feels emotions *because* of his thoughts. Thoughts create emotions and perceptions, not the other way around. Therefore, your child's inner thoughts have everything to do with his emotional state!

While an external event might trigger your child's anxiety, negative self-talk is what maintains and often feeds the anxiety. Worry is self-generated by dwelling on worst-case scenarios, planning obsessively about what to do in a situation that has not yet happened, avoiding situations that might be negative, thinking about the negatives in a situation while ignoring the positives, and so on. As the Roman Emperor Marcus Aurelius said, "We are disturbed not by things but by our perception of things."

How can I help my child reduce negative self-talk?

With the right plan, your child can learn to control her thoughts and mitigate her worries and anxiety. First teach her to be mindful about her body's signals that she is experiencing prolonged anxiety—rapid breathing, tightness in the chest, upset stomach. Explain that when she feels these symptoms, she is likely engaging in negative self-talk. She can then choose to take action to get out of that negative mode. Switching from worry mode to action mode will help her feel more hopeful. Just having a plan in itself can lessen anxiety. It will help her reset and access her prefrontal cortex.

Some techniques you can teach your child include challenging negative thoughts, building a store of positive thoughts, keeping a gratitude journal, and using "I statements" to defuse triggering situations. By using these tools, your child will learn to understand the difference between productive and unproductive worrying, which is crucial. She will get to the point where she believes that "what if" thoughts are unproductive, worrying does not help, and the worst-case scenarios playing in her mind are not true.

How can my child challenge negative thoughts?

Worries tend to stick around if you pay attention to them. Feeding worry with constant negative self-talk ensures the worry will return. One strategy for breaking this cycle is to challenge negative thoughts as they appear. To help your child learn to do so, first explain that the brain can make mistakes as it tries to protect him. The brain sometimes perceives normal things as being dangerous, but he has the choice to question his thoughts to make sure they are accurate.

Once your child believes that his thoughts aren't necessarily true and accurate, encourage him to examine his next negative thought and to challenge it. Use the questions in *Challenging Negative Thoughts* on page 98 to help him. The idea is for him to be able to move from thinking, *This is awful. I can't handle this*, to, *This isn't as bad as my brain thinks it is. It's okay. I can handle it.*

With practice, your child can learn to calm himself and replace negative self-talk with positive thoughts. For example, if he has an anxiety attack when he is about to take a test, he can first identify what negative self-talk is causing the anxiety: *I'm stupid. I'm going to fail!* Then he can remind himself: *Just because I am thinking this, doesn't mean it's true. Is this worry legitimate or is it a false alarm?* He can remind himself that his brain does not know the difference between a tiger and a minor stressor like the test in front of him. Then he can challenge his negative thoughts: *Am I really stupid? What evidence do I have for that? If I do fail, is failing the end of the world? Is it something I can handle?* Next he can ask himself, *What can I say to myself instead?* Finally, he can replace his inner dialogue with positive, encouraging thoughts: *I am smart. I studied for this test. I have done well on all my other tests, so I will probably do well on this one. If I don't do well, my life is not over. I will simply get help studying for the next one.*

What does it mean to build a store of positive thoughts?

Because of the brain's negativity bias, humans are predisposed to an imbalance between negative and positive thoughts. One way to shift the scale is to purposefully build a store of positive mental images and feelings. Focusing on only the positive in life is not realistic, but making a conscious effort to notice and appreciate the positive creates feelings of gratitude, which can, in turn, significantly improve mood and build resilience to stress.

Encourage your child to look for the positive in her life. Explain that by acknowledging and enjoying positive things, she can actually change the circuitry in her brain. She will have a more calm inner strength to control her anxiety. When she experiences a positive moment, she should take a little longer than usual to enjoy it. Encourage her to *create* positive moments, like cuddling with her pet or watching a funny show or hanging out with her friend in her room. Teach her to be intentional about noticing not only what is WRONG (her arm hurts) but also what is RIGHT (the rest of her body is strong and pain-free, she has less homework than usual, and her friend

47

bought her a gift today to cheer her up). See *Creating Positivity* on page 99 for reminders on how to build a store of positive thoughts.

Tell me about gratitude journals. Are they useful with preteens?

An excellent stress-management tool for a preteen is keeping a gratitude journal—a notebook in which he records daily the things that make him happy or things he is grateful for. Note that this is different than a typical diary or journal, in which he might describe negative things that happened that day or his negative thoughts and fears. At this age, writing about the negative does not usually help.

Asking your preteen to pause and enter positive thoughts into a journal helps him focus on the positive and on what is going right in his life, which in turn creates a feeling of gratitude. This is another way to build his store of positive thoughts. The idea is to get him in the habit of focusing on the positive and to teach him the value of reflection and showing gratitude.

As your child gets into the habit of writing in his gratitude journal, he will be more open to expressing gratitude in his everyday life. Remind him to show gratitude toward his family as well as to members of his community, such as his teachers and coaches, the mail carrier, and the staff at his favorite restaurant. Remind him gently with caring words, such as, "Miss Amanda worked really hard to make these delicious pancakes for you." Showing gratitude is a way of connecting with others, which adds to a child's sense of safety and self-worth. The reaction alone of the recipient of the gratitude can frequently change your child's disposition and serve as a great distracter from his worries.

Encourage your child to keep a gratitude journal by his bed, perhaps in his nightstand, and to write in it every day. He can choose to lock his gratitude journal if privacy is important to him. Using a paper journal, versus an online journal on the computer, is preferred (unless there is an issue with fine motor skills) because the act of writing stimulates and engages the brain more effectively than typing. Committing to a regular schedule, like at bedtime just before he turns the lights out, will help writing in it to become a habit. Remind your child to write in his journal, but be flexible if he misses at times. If he seems to be stuck, give a simple, impersonal hint: "Today I had the most amazing ice cream at a new place." Occasionally reward him for his effort, for example, by giving him a special pen or a treat. If your child needs help building the practice of writing in a gratitude journal, refer to the tips in *Keeping a Gratitude Journal* on page 95.

What are "I statements" and how can they diffuse triggering situations?

Communication among siblings in the home can serve as a frequent trigger to anxiety and negative self-talk. For example, two teenagers in a family I worked with were doing homework.

The teenage son finished first and began bragging about it and teasing his younger sister for being slow. Suddenly the sister threw her workbook at her brother, hitting him in the face and almost breaking his glasses. He got mad and started yelling at her. She, in turn, became even more furious and yelled back at him. When the dad talked to his daughter, he learned that she initially tried to ignore her brother's comments, but as her brother continued teasing her, her "what ifs" took over. *What if he really is smarter than me? What if I don't do well and have to go to summer school? What if I have to repeat my grade?* She could not think of a comeback, she felt restless, her head felt like it was about to burst, and her heart was pounding. She explained she threw the workbook almost without thinking, not intending to hurt him.

All siblings quarrel, some more than others. When the quarreling gets out of control, parents often tell their children to apologize, but this typically leaves the children still feeling upset. A much more effective strategy is to coach your child to use "I statements," ideally as soon as she begins to feel triggered. "I statements" are a way of communicating feelings without being judgmental or confrontational. You tell the person who is upsetting you how his behavior makes you feel and what you would like him to do instead (as opposed to a "you statement" that tells him what he is doing wrong, labels him, or judges him). In this case the sister could have told her brother, "I feel hurt when you make fun of me and tease me about being a slowpoke. Please don't do that again," instead of throwing her workbook or yelling at him, "You're always so mean!"

Explain and teach your child to use "I statements." Model using them yourself. "I feel angry when I have to clean up your room so frequently. I expect you to work with me." When you hear your child make a "you statement," gently remind her to rephrase with an "I statement." With practice, you both will begin using "I statements" more and more automatically, and your communication will become more and more effective. See *Using "I Statements"* on page 107 for more examples.

While "I statements" are effective at diffusing a situation before it gets out of control, they can also help after a situation blows up. The dad in this family coached his daughter to write a note using "I statements," explaining how she felt during the incident. He then discussed with her more productive ways she could have communicated with her brother in the moment. Together they decided she would initiate a reconciliation by doing something nice for her brother, such as bringing him a snack or a drink, sharing her music with him, or offering to play a video game with him—and even sharing her note with him. Sharing her thoughts and worries with her brother, someone she cares about, made her feel a lot better. She realized she didn't have to be alone in her worries. It also gave him the opportunity to think of ways to help her and possibly avoid repeating his triggering behavior in the future.

CHAPTER 7
The Avoidance Pitfall

You love your child. You want the best for him and you'd do anything for him. When he is in danger or in pain, you protect him. So when you see him suffering from anxiety, your natural inclination is to try to make it all better. One strategy you might be employing is trying to identify triggers that exacerbate his anxiety and then helping him avoid those triggers. Anticipating your child's fears to help him avoid uncomfortable situations is a common (and quite understandable) pitfall of parents with anxious kids.

What's wrong with avoiding triggers that cause my child anxiety?

One practical problem with the "avoid triggers" strategy is that it is not a long-term solution. It might be effective for a while, but new anxiety-producing situations will continue to come up, and you will find it more and more difficult to protect your child. At some point, it will be impossible to avoid all stressors.

Another problem with the avoidance technique is that it reinforces anxiety. Helping your child avoid situations she is afraid of makes her feel better in the moment, but in doing so, you are also sending her the message, "This situation really is bad and frightening. You can't cope so you better avoid it." The next time a similar situation arises, she is very likely to use avoidance again as her coping strategy. The cycle repeats itself until she is more and more isolated and anxious. For example, imagine taking your child to a birthday party where she clings to you and doesn't want you to leave. As you encourage her to interact and have fun, after a few minutes she is back, looks upset, and asks you to take her home. If you go along with it, you are in effect telling her, "You're right, parties with a lot of people are scary and dangerous. You can't handle it. We should leave." The next time she begins to feel anxious in a crowded environment, she will want to leave again because that's how the two of you solved the problem last time.

If avoiding triggers doesn't work, then how should I help my child?

A more effective strategy is to help your child learn to handle the discomfort that comes with anxiety as well as possible. By sitting with his anxiety and tolerating the discomfort instead of seeking avoidance and running away, he will experience less anxiety over time. To be clear, there *is* value in helping your child identify situations that trigger anxiety—but not for the purpose of avoiding them. The purpose is to be prepared to handle his anxiety when he finds himself in those situations.

How can I help my child learn to tolerate her anxiety?

Challenge your child to move toward the discomfort she is feeling in small, gradual steps. Begin by using verbal encouragement to coach her through the experience so she can be prepared to handle it. First acknowledge her fears. For example, "I know you're scared, but that's okay. I'm here and I can help you through this." It might be tempting to explain why she has nothing to fear. "Don't worry, you won't fail," or "Nobody is going to make fun of you at your class presentation." Avoid this mistake. Dismissing her feelings will put her in that much more of an anxious state.

Next, encourage her to talk about her feelings by asking open-ended questions, such as "How are you feeling about your upcoming science test?" Avoid asking leading questions that might amplify her fear, like, "Are you anxious about taking your science test today?"

Finally, acknowledge the work it takes for her to tolerate her anxiety. Make sure she knows you are noticing how hard she is working and how much you are appreciating her efforts.

As you coach your child, periodically express your confidence that she is going to be all right, that it will only get better, and above all, she will be able to manage it. This continuous encouragement will give her confidence. She will feel reassured knowing you believe she is capable of getting through it.

As your verbal encouragement becomes more and more effective at getting your child to communicate her feelings through discussions with you, then you can move toward setting up specific challenges with incentives for her efforts.

What do you mean by incentives?

The idea is to target specific behaviors you want your child to demonstrate, develop a behavior plan, and give him a tangible reward or privilege when he demonstrates that behavior. This is fairly easy to implement with a young child. "If you pick up your toys before bedtime every weekday, you get 30 extra minutes of television on the weekend." Implementing incentives with preteens is more challenging, but it works.

Begin by asking your child what he worries about most, and target that fear first. Together set up a ladder hierarchy that includes small steps he can take that will lead to ultimately facing that particular fear. As he moves toward his discomfort gradually with each step, his fear will lessen, eventually allowing him to face it and go through it. If separation anxiety is his primary fear, for example, the list might read something like:

- Get plenty of sleep.
- Start the day with a healthy breakfast.
- Take a 15-minute walk around the neighborhood each day for stress relief.
- Practice deep, slow breathing exercises each day.

- Discuss the possibility of staying at a friend's house for 30 minutes. (Ask him, "What would that be like? How worried would you feel on a scale from 1 to 10?")
- Make plans with a friend for a short visit.
- Practice breathing exercises 10 minutes before the visit.
- Visit the friend for 30 minutes.
- Call a friend and talk about a TV program or movie that you watched recently and liked.
- Invite a friend to your house to play games or watch a movie.
- Plan a sleepover with a friend.

As you discuss the incentive plan with your child, acknowledge to him that his anxiety might come back even after he goes through the steps. Explain the goal is to work through his fears and to practice coping strategies, so that the next time the anxiety returns, he is a little more able to manage it. It is a process, not a one-time magical solution. Together you might also decide in advance on a tangible reward he will receive as he moves through the hierarchy of steps. Perhaps he gets a point for each step he completes successfully, and when he has earned a certain number of points, he receives a new game or his favorite meal. Choose something that you are willing to award and he is excited about earning.

Most importantly, as your child works through his list, make sure he sees the steps he is taking and the benefits he is experiencing along the way. You might opt to draw a ladder diagram, with the first item at the bottom and the last item at the top, so he has a visual for the progress he is making as he "climbs the ladder." Work on at least one challenge a day—more if he's showing motivation and a willingness to try. If he begins to get anxious any time throughout the process, remind him to practice one of the calming strategies he has learned to keep his cortisol level in check.

What is the best way to motivate my child to keep going and to support her efforts?

As a parent and as a professional working with children, my motto has always been, "Notice the positive and praise often!" However, in the course of your busy day, you might fall into the habit of giving your child a quick "good job." Not only does that overused phrase feel meaningless to your child when she does something she is really proud of, but it also is an evaluative comment—it implies judgment when you label something as "good" or "bad."

Psychologists and educators suggest that instead of making evaluative comments about your children's positive behaviors, using more specific, descriptive praise might be more effective in helping your child recognize the benefit of her effort and hard work. Descriptive praise focuses on the whole process—her effort, choices, and attitude toward the task—regardless of the outcome. This serves as a better motivator for your child and contributes to a healthier self-esteem. Using descriptive phrases takes more time and effort on your part. It requires recognizing what your child has done and how her actions are beneficial to her or others.

For example, instead of saying, "That's an awesome painting," you can say, "I can see you worked hard on that painting. I like the colors you used." Instead of saying, "Great job," you can say, "Thank you for helping me make dinner. We worked together and got it done much faster." For more examples of descriptive praise, see *Using Descriptive Praise* on page 80.

CHAPTER 8
Parental Stress

Most parents feel a certain amount of stress in their day-to-day lives; that is normal. However, life sometimes becomes more difficult, causing stress levels to soar. Facing unpredictable events makes parents more susceptible to excessive worrying and anxiety. For example, adults are becoming increasingly anxious as they deal with the current COVID-19 pandemic and the impact it has on their finances and family life.

What does my stress level have to do with my anxious child?

Parental stress has a direct impact on a child's anxiety level. Children generally tune in to their parents' moods under normal circumstances. When parental stress spikes, it becomes much more noticeable to children and can trigger their own overactive amygdala, leaving them feeling that there is a real threat. Kids today are smarter, more intuitive, and more curious than ever before in our history as a nation. They have better problem-solving abilities and are certainly more media savvy than most adults. When they hear their parents talking in the background, they notice. They sense their parents' worry. They do not want to ask questions or initiate discussions because they want to avoid upsetting their parents even more. This makes them feel alone, and having to manage their feelings alone causes them stress. Very often, their imaginations take over, creating scenarios that are worse than reality, overwhelming their young minds and bodies.

I cannot control the circumstances causing my stress. So what can I do about it?

Though you cannot always reduce the amount of stress you are feeling, you can mitigate the impact of that stress on your child. Be mindful of your own stress level and excessive worrying. When you are going through a particularly stressful situation, have an honest discussion with your child. Do not overwhelm him with too much detail, but let him know what is going on, that the adults are in control and figuring out what to do, and that he can delegate his worries to you.

I don't want to overwhelm my child. How much detail should I share?

Start with an overall honest explanation of the situation. For example, "Dad was laid off from his job today, but he is well-trained and has a lot of experience and will start looking right away for new opportunities. In the meantime, we have to cut down on our spending and try to be helpful to each other around the house and stay positive." Then allow your children to ask questions. Use their questions as a guide for how much more information to give them about what is happening.

Young children absorb information in small chunks. They ask questions, listen to what you have to say, and go off to play. When they are ready to hear more, they come back with more questions.

Preteens generally have more questions right away, and since they are capable of more logical thinking and judgment, they are able to absorb and process more detailed information. As they learn, they tend to gain a sense of control and feel less fear.

When my child has an anxiety attack, my stress level spikes. What can I do in the moment?

Before engaging with your upset child, regulating your own stress response is important. Calm yourself so you can calm your child. Your child will often do what you do and feel what you feel, so you want to engage with her calmly to avoid escalating her anxiety. This might mean leaving the room momentarily, talking about the situation with someone else before approaching your child, or simply taking four or five deep, slow breaths. When you do engage with your child, be mindful of your tone of voice, your facial expression, and your body posture. Try to project a confident, calm demeanor. Use positive language whenever possible. For example, say "have fun" instead of "be careful." Point out coping behaviors you have noticed your child using successfully, such as, "School has been tough this week, but you hung in there and learned a lot."

CHAPTER 9
You Can Do It!

nxiety is rampant in today's world, especially among preteens and teens. Watching your child go through physical and mental anguish is difficult, to say the least. You probably feel frightened, worried, and at a loss as to how to help him. You might be constantly on alert for his particular triggers, exerting a lot of mental and emotional energy in helping him avoid them. You might be frustrated at seemingly defiant behavior and trying different methods of discipline.

As a parent, sometimes the most difficult step is the first step—accepting that your child has a serious condition that needs intervention, and then committing to be part of the solution. When anxiety becomes so intense that it is seriously affecting your child's life and the family, you must seek ways you can help.

Since you have taken the time to read Part One of this book, you are well on your way to making a positive difference in your child's life. I encourage you not to stop now. Studies demonstrate that low-intensity therapeutic approaches for children with anxiety disorders, particularly brief, parent-guided strategies, can be quite effective. Children can overcome problems before the problems become so severe that they require specialists and more high-intensity interventions. With the right strategies, you *can* help your child learn to cope with and work toward overcoming his anxiety.

Before going any further, make that first step: accept that your child needs your help and commit to being part of the solution. Begin by following the advice in Part One of this book. Have an open conversation with your child about what anxiety is, how it looks and feels, the role the brain plays, and why false alarms happen. Make sure he (and you!) knows that anxiety is not his fault, and that you are going to help him learn to manage it. When he has an episode, discuss what happened in terms of the three parts of anxiety: anxious thoughts, physical symptoms, and avoidance behaviors. Explain the value of using strategies to tolerate and get through anxiety versus strategies to avoid anxiety. Show him that he has a large set of tools at his disposal, outlined in *Toolkit of Brain-Smart Strategies* on page 71 and assure him that the more he practices them, the more his anxiety will lessen.

Then use Part Two as you begin coaching him to practice the strategies. Go slowly so he is not overwhelmed. Try different ones to learn what works best for you, him, and your family. Use the *Strategy Log* section to make notes. Consider reading a few other resources in *Additional Resources for Parents and Preteens* to learn even more about anxiety. Last but not least, as you work with your child, use some of the parent strategies to manage your own stress. Practice the relaxation strategies with him, which will help you and has the added benefit of being a bonding experience. If you are worried about something, talk to him about it instead of pretending nothing is wrong. (A kid knows when something is up, and his imagination is usually worse than reality!) Strive to be a role model. I'm sure you have discovered that kids do not do as we say but do as we do.

My hope is that after reading this book you will come away feeling more optimistic, less worried, and extremely motivated to begin working with your child. Making a commitment to go through this journey with him will be highly gratifying for all of you. You can do it!

PART
TWO

Toolkit of Brain-Smart Strategies

You have multiple strategies to choose from when coaching your preteen to move through his anxiety. The most important thing to understand and accept is that not all strategies are effective for everyone. You must practice numerous strategies to figure out what works best for you and your child. We all process information differently; some people are auditory learners (listening), some are kinesthetic learners (doing), and some are visual learners (observing). Each of these learning modalities utilizes a different pathway to the brain, so trying different approaches is essential. It takes time and trial and error to reach success.

When you anticipate a situation might cause an anxiety attack, remind your child to try some of the brain-smart strategies in this chapter. Try some of the parent strategies as well. As you and your child test strategies, mark the ones that are helpful in the following list for future reference. For those that are helpful, record more information about the experience in the *Strategy Log* section on page 111.

Parent Strategies

👍 👎 Modeling Calm Behavior (p. 74)

👍 👎 Determining When Anxiety Is a Problem (p. 74)

👍 👎 Teaching Your Child about Anxiety (p. 76)

👍 👎 Connecting with Your Child (p. 77)

👍 👎 Disciplining in a Nonaggressive Manner (p. 77)

👍 👎 Keeping a United Front (p. 78)

👍 👎 Teaching Project Management (p. 79)

👍 👎 Modeling and Encouraging Humor (p. 79)

👍 👎 Using Descriptive Praise (p. 80)

👍 👎 Avoiding Rushing Your Child (p. 81)

👍 👎 Preparing Your Child for New Experiences (p. 81)

👍 👎 Using the Power of Human Touch (p. 82)

👍 👎 Waiting for the Calm After the Storm (p. 83)

👍 👎 Teaching Your Child Brain-Smart Strategies (p. 84)

👍 👎 Implementing Informal School Interventions (p. 85)

👍 👎 Requesting a 504 Plan (p. 86)

👍 👎 Seeking Help When Needed (p. 89)

Proactive Strategies

👍 👎 Establishing an Exercise Routine (p. 92)

👍 👎 Establishing a Relaxation Routine (p. 92)

👍 👎 Minimizing Distractions when Studying (p. 93)

👍 👎 Planning Activities in Advance (p. 94)

👍 👎 Setting a Bedtime Routine (p. 94)

👍 👎 Keeping a Gratitude Journal (p. 95)

Panic Attack Strategies

👍 👎 Using Distractions (p. 96)

👍 👎 Engaging in Repetitive Movement (p. 97)

👍 👎 Engaging in Bursts of Exercise (p. 98)

👍 👎 Challenging Negative Thoughts (p. 98)

👍 👎 Creating Positivity (p. 99)

👍 👎 Relaxing in Your Own Cave (p. 99)

👍 👎 Using Visualization and Guided Imagery (p. 100)

👍 👎 Doing Belly Breathing Exercises (p. 101)

👍 👎 Doing Progressive Relaxation Exercises (p. 102)

👍 👎 Using Scent as a Relaxation Tool (p. 105)

Communication Strategies

👍 👎 Setting Family Rules Together (p. 106)

👍 👎 Practicing Communicating Feelings (p. 106)

👍 👎 Using "I Statements" (p. 107)

👍 👎 Not Avoiding Difficult Conversations (p. 107)

👍 👎 Listening Closely (p. 108)

Parent Strategies

Parents often ask what they can do to help their children who are experiencing excessive worrying, which often leads to debilitating anxious states. These are strategies you can practice yourself to create a calm, positive atmosphere in your home and to lessen the likelihood of your child having panic attacks. You can start helping your children by implementing these strategies.

Modeling Calm Behavior

First and foremost, model being calm yourself. Use challenging times as opportunities to show your child appropriate, constructive ways to handle an over-activated nervous system during tough situations. This provides a positive, proactive, supportive, and safe home environment for your child. When the difficult situation involves your child, staying calm helps them to stay calm as well.

Determining When Anxiety Is a Problem

As parents, we know a certain level of worry in children is normal and is not harmful when it happens occasionally. But if the worrying cannot be managed by your child, is triggered by minor events or thoughts, and is beginning to become all-consuming, it can negatively impact your child's health and can cause social and academic barriers. This is the time for you to step in and address the problem. Early intervention and skill building in handling excessive worrying are the best gifts you can give your child. However, recognizing when your child has moved beyond normal worrying into excessive worrying can be difficult, especially when the transition happens gradually. The following are signs that your child is struggling with anxiety and probably needs intervention:

- Frequent complaints of headaches, nausea, stomachaches, or fatigue, with no medical reason
- Too many "what ifs" and a preoccupation with bad things happening
- Restlessness and irritability
- Trouble sleeping, frequent waking during the night, or nightmares
- Crying, whining, anger, or extreme sensitivity without a clear reason
- Rapid heart rate and/or breathing
- Sudden difficulty separating from parents
- Refusal to go to school
- Attention and memory problems
- Lack of participation in important social events
- Perfectionism
- Frequent meltdowns and temper tantrums
- Sudden bedwetting
- Motor tics, such as uncontrolled blinking, tapping, or noises

Teaching Your Child About Anxiety

Before your child can work on getting through her anxiety, she must first understand what is happening to her. Start a dialogue with her that explains anxiety, helps her recognize the symptoms, and encourages her to talk about her fears. Show acceptance and acknowledgment of her worries and anxious feelings.

- Teach her about anxiety and how to recognize it.
- Explain that anxiety has physiological causes to encourage her to become more aware of the sensations in her body.
- Help her to label her feelings.
- Explain the fight, flight, or freeze response using *What is the best way to explain fight, flight, or freeze to preteens?* on p. 27 as your guide.
- Explain anxiety can be hereditary.
- Explain even if there is no family history of anxiety, anxiety can develop after a traumatic event.
- Share things you were overly worried about at her age.
- Encourage her to share what she is worried about.
- Describe a recent situation in which she was exhibiting signs of extreme anxiety.
- Periodically reassure her that her feelings are okay.
- Remain calm to encourage her to feel calm.
- Remind her that though anxiety is uncomfortable, it doesn't last long, is treatable, and is not dangerous.

Connecting with Your Child

In order for your child to trust you and open up to you, you must build an emotional connection with her. Smile often. Notice when she does something nice or helpful and say thank you. Be deliberate about creating opportunities for connection. You can go on walks together, talk, play games, participate in a sport, paint each other's nails, cook a meal together, and so on. If you notice she made an exceptional effort or had a particularly challenging week, surprise her with a special treat when she least expects it. Take a trip to the ice cream shop, perhaps, or make her favorite meal or allow her to invite a friend for a sleepover. Let her know you noticed her effort.

Disciplining in a Nonaggressive Manner

Anxious kids tend to be overly sensitive perfectionists. They generally want to do the right thing and make their parents happy. When you raise your voice and act in an aggressive manner, they might feel nervous. If you are stern or overly punitive when you discipline, they are quick to feel they are not liked or not good enough. Try these strategies when disciplining your anxious child:

- Wait until you are calm to address the wrongdoing. Telling your child you will talk about what he has done in an hour or tomorrow is better than talking about it immediately while angry or tearful.
- When you are ready, sit down with your child to discuss the situation. Maintain a calm, loving tone of voice. If he

is still upset or angry, give him more time. You can say, "I can see you have strong feelings about this. Let's take some more time to relax and think and we'll talk about it later." Do not proceed with your talk until he is calm.

- Use value-based discipline to set rules and expectations without embarrassment or judgment; that is, focus on the *value* involved in the situation, not on what is "right" or "wrong." Remind him that as a family you value kindness, respect, gratitude, etc. For example, if he lied about doing homework or breaking something, talk about the value of honesty and the importance of not violating trust in your family.

- Ask him what he was feeling when he committed the wrongdoing. If he has trouble labeling his emotion, help him identify it.

- Validate the way he was feeling, but make it clear you disapprove of the way he demonstrated it. Tell him you still love him no matter what.

- Discuss what he could have done instead. Stay on topic and do not bring up past inappropriate behaviors.

- Reassure him often that he is capable and loved.

Keeping a United Front

As parents, show a united front on how you handle a particular situation. You certainly can disagree with each other, but disagree privately; otherwise, your children might take advantage of your disagreement and become more defiant.

Teaching Project Management

Many children become anxious and overwhelmed when faced with a large project. Teach your child to break up large projects into smaller, less intimidating tasks she can tackle one at a time. If your child shuts down at the prospect of cleaning up her disastrously messy room, for example, encourage her to focus on putting all dirty clothes in the hamper first, then folding clean clothes and putting them in her dresser, then straightening up her desk, then empting her garbage, and so on.

Modeling how to do a project is a very effective approach as well. For example, take a Saturday morning to work together with your child to clean and organize her room, verbalizing each step as you go. When you are done, take a picture of the room, print it, and tape it to her door. Next time you ask her to clean and organize her room, if she picks up a few things and then tells you she is done, point to the picture on her door and ask, "Does your room look like this picture yet?" If the answer is no, tell her to keep working on it. This takes away the argument and places the responsibility on your child.

Modeling and Encouraging Humor

Laughter is a wonderful stress reliever that can soothe muscle tension and help the body relax. It can be highly therapeutic, and it is a great way to engage family members to talk and share about their day. Emphasize and model humor for your child.

- Have each family member take turns sharing a joke during dinner. Encourage your child to prepare by looking online for jokes by kids before dinner.
- Create a bulletin board where the family can post funny photos, comic strips, memes, etc.
- Try not to take the little things too seriously. For example, if someone accidentally spills the milk, instead of yelling or blaming, make a light-hearted joke as you clean it up together. "If you didn't want milk tonight, you could have just told me!"

Using Descriptive Praise

Praise your child sincerely and often, but avoid using evaluative praise like, "Good job!" Instead, use more specific, descriptive praise, such as:

- Thank you for helping.
- It was difficult but you did not give up!
- I can tell you really enjoyed that game.
- You are being an extremely helpful and kind friend or sister.
- I can see you are concentrating awfully hard.
- I can tell you tried your hardest.
- You did it!
- I can see all your practice is paying off.
- It looks like you've been working very diligently.
- I can tell you are really enjoying soccer.

- What do you like best about your work?
- Thanks for waiting so patiently.

Avoiding Rushing Your Child

Life is busy; rushing from one thing to another is a habit that is easy to slip into. However, children need some down time in their lives, and they require more time than adults to process verbal directions and to transition from one activity to another. Preparing your child for transitions will go a long way in minimizing her worrying and her fight, flight, or freeze response.

- Avoid overscheduling your child. Do not allow her to participate in so many activities that there is no down time at home.
- Give your child advance notice when you want her to do a task. "Dinner will be ready in 20 minutes. Please set the table before then."
- Give your child a 10-minute reminder with a brief explanation before she has to go somewhere. "Remember you have gymnastics practice at 5:00 today. To allow time for traffic, we need to leave in 10 minutes."

Preparing Your Child for New Experiences

Children often become anxious when trying something new, going somewhere alone, or participating in crowded events. If your child is going to experience an event that typically causes him anxiety, rather than avoiding the experience, give him information about what to expect in advance. This way he will be mentally prepared and ready to use strategies to get through it. Some frequent anxiety-inducing stressors include:

- Going to a new school, especially the first day
- Making new friends
- Trying a new sport or activity
- Speaking in front of people
- Experiencing parental conflict
- Taking important tests
- Lacking private time or personal quiet time
- Moving often and changing schools
- Going through the divorce and remarriage of parents
- Having a new baby in the family
- Being exposed to frequent bullying
- Struggling with learning problems and unrealistic expectations from adults
- Not feeling accepted by peers
- Being overloaded with homework
- Frequently worrying about appearance
- Trying to gain acceptance from peers

Using the Power of Human Touch

Research shows that children feel happier, are less fidgety, and stay calmer when given a soothing touch. Newborns instinctively crave it, and older children are quickly comforted when held lovingly, caressed, rocked, or hugged in their parents' arms. Think of every touch like a little gift that you give your child and, certainly, to yourself as well.

- Make a point to touch your child often. For example, when you want your child's attention and you want to encourage eye contact, gently touch his cheek.

- Give your child hugs often. It brings more joy to your family life.

- When you hug your child, tighten your grasp and really snuggle. Close your eyes, breathe deeply, and focus on the feeling of your arms around him. You will both feel emotionally closer to each other.

- Encourage your child to give himself a hug when you are not around. Say, "I love giving myself a big bear hug, too." Encourage him to try it with you.

- Give your child a back massage or another tactile relaxing experience, like scratching his back, lightly "tickling" his arm, massaging his head and neck, and the like.

Waiting for the Calm After the Storm

Trying to reason with children when they are upset or angry fosters a fight, flight, or freeze response. Approaching them with logic or anger when they are in the middle of a panic attack only escalates their anxiety and worrying, as well as yours. Instead, when your child is upset and anxious, lovingly remind her to use some of the brain-smart strategies listed in the rest of this chapter to get her through it. Once she is calm, then you can talk to her about the event, being sure to praise calm behavior and her effort instead of criticizing her negative actions.

- Validate her feelings while letting her know her actions were inappropriate. "I understand why you were angry, and it's normal to feel like hurting someone when you're angry, but you know it's not okay to get physical where you can hurt yourself or someone else."
- You can discuss consequences for her actions, but avoid focusing on the negative, for example, on the fact that she was screaming, cursing, or throwing things.
- Brainstorm what she can do in the same situation next time.
- Focus on the positive, such as that she was able to eventually calm herself down or perhaps she was able to self-soothe and become calm more quickly than usual.
- Talk about what might have triggered her anxiety.
- If appropriate, challenge her negative thoughts. For example, if she says, "No one wants to be my friend," you might point out kind gestures from others such as a classmate inviting her to a birthday party or a friend making room for her to sit at a table for lunch in the crowded cafeteria.

Teaching Your Child Brain-Smart Strategies

Of course, to help your child cope with anxiety, not only is it important to work on these parenting strategies yourself, but you also must teach your child coping skills he can use to manage and take control of his anxiety. Take the time to educate and empower yourself on the strategies described in the rest of this chapter. Teach and coach your child on the different options. Allow him time to practice these skills without fear of consequences or punishment for his constant "what ifs," fears, and worries. Practice the strategies with him until they become habits and he can do them on his own. While you cannot control what anxiety your child will face each day, you can give him tools to help him control the way he responds.

Implementing Informal School Interventions

While you are coaching your child to use brain-smart strategies, it is important to minimize his anxiety on school days as much as possible. You can help him by implementing these strategies:

- Bring him to school early.
- Be patient and avoid rushing him.
- Help him prepare his backpack and school material each night, placing it by the door so it is ready to go when he leaves the next morning.

But you can also help by involving his teachers, guidance counselor, and school psychologist. Ask school personnel to be as supportive as possible and to listen to your child's concerns without minimizing his feelings. Request that they implement some of the following interventions for him in the classroom (Huberty, 2010).

- Provide him time to relax and do breathing exercises when his anxiety becomes too high.
- Avoid punitive and negative attitudes.
- Reduce time constraints when possible.
- Provide seating in a quiet place with fewer distractions.
- Break tasks into smaller, more manageable chunks.
- Set clear and reasonable expectations.

Requesting a 504 Plan

Section 504 of the Rehabilitation Act of 1973 was created to prevent discrimination in the classroom due to disabilities, and anxiety disorder qualifies as a disability. If the informal accommodations you set up with your child's teacher and school team have not been sufficient in meeting his needs, do not hesitate to request an assessment to determine if your child qualifies for a 504 Plan. Use this law as a means to advocate for your child. The intention is not to change *what* she learns but rather *how* she learns

To request such a plan, speak to your child's teacher, guidance counselor, and school psychologist. The first step is for a psychologist or psychiatrist to conduct a formal assessment to determine if your child meets the criteria for an anxiety disorder. If she is diagnosed with an anxiety disorder, the next step is for the school team to have planning meetings to determine which of the available accommodations are appropriate for her. Make every effort to attend these meetings so you can participate in the planning. Some classroom-based accommodations available under the 504 Plan are as follows:

- Provide preferential seating in the classroom. Seat student away from areas that might stimulate anxiety, such as a window or next to the teacher where students frequently go to ask questions.
- Present directions verbally and in writing so the student can double-check that she understands expectations.
- Allow student the option to be exempt when students are answering questions on the board or in front of the class.
- Assign a buddy to student during lunch, recess, and/or unstructured activities, if student agrees.
- Allow student to leave the classroom without permission so she can go to the restroom for small breaks when feeling tense or anxious.
- Allow student to leave the classroom with permission when feeling tense or anxious to talk to a mentor/teacher who might be designated in advance.
- Give student the choice of seating in large group settings, such as during presentations in the gym or auditorium.
- Provide prior notification, if possible, before a substantial change in student's daily routine, such as a substitute teacher instructing the class.
- Pair student with a teacher or aide during field trips, or invite student's parents to attend.

- Provide prior notification, if possible, of fire drills, and place student with a mentor/teacher to minimize anxiety.
- Allow student to use a recording device in the classroom to record lectures or discussions if she is unable to keep up with note taking.
- Allow student to chew gum to reduce tension, when appropriate.
- Provide student a bouncy chair that allows for repetitive movement while seated.
- Incorporate a variety of lesson presentation avenues, such as small-group lessons, large-group lessons, computer-based lessons, etc.
- Post a checklist for daily routines in the classroom to make student's day more predictable.
- Provide student opportunities for socialization by setting up cooperative situations in the classroom, such as assigning small groups to work together and playing games together.
- Provide explanations in small distinct steps and give clear directions for each section separately.
- Use non-verbal signals or cues to refocus student to task.
- Place focus on student's effort and process when working on a task, not on the end result.
- Give student extra time to complete classroom assignments, classroom tests, and standardized tests.

- Give student some important responsibility in the classroom so that she has a chance to connect with her classmates (e.g., distributing or collecting papers and tests).
- Let student know in advance, preferably at least the day before, when she is going to be called to get up in front of her peers (e.g., when she will be called to the board or have to give a class presentation).
- Provide testing in small groups.
- Provide student a set of notes if she is having trouble getting everything written down in class.

Seeking Help When Needed

Do not be afraid to ask for help from a professional when nothing else is working. If you do not see sufficient progress with your child even after extensive practice of these brain-smart strategies, consider seeking treatment from a licensed healthcare professional.

- A psychologist has the expertise to make a full assessment of your child and use therapeutic approaches. Research over the past 20 years shows the cognitive behavior therapy (CBT) approach is the most effective treatment for reducing symptoms of severe anxiety. Unlike talk therapy, in which the therapist and child try to get to the root of the anxiety in an attempt to change behavior, CBT aims to change behavior to deal with the fear. CBT involves identifying triggers; exposing the child to the triggers in structured, incremental steps; and challenging the child's worries and assumptions.

- A psychiatrist can determine if your child is a candidate for medication. However, please note that anxiety in preteens is best managed with consistent therapy and knowledge, whenever possible, due to the side effects of medication. If your child takes medication, absolutely do not stop the medication without the advice of a physician; abruptly discontinuing some medications is harmful.

- A neurologist can provide or prescribe neurofeedback training for your child, which has been known to improve cognitive function, attention, mood, anxiety, sleep, and behavior. Often referred to as brain training, neurofeedback is used to help children learn to manage their brain activity, such as their breathing, heart rate, and muscle contractions, without the use of medication. Noninvasive sensors that read brainwaves are placed on the child's head, and the brainwaves are displayed on a computer screen. This biofeedback is then used to train the child to quiet her mind, control stress, and not overreact, often through playing video games.

All these treatment options should be done in close consultation with your family physician and coordinated with your child's school. Teachers and school psychologists have the opportunity and expertise to closely observe your child in action in the course of the school day and provide you with valuable information on her daily functioning and progress dealing with anxiety.

Proactive Strategies

These are strategies that set up your child for success and lessen the likelihood of panic attacks. Coach your child on adopting them into his everyday life, giving gentle reminders at first, until they become routine.

Establishing an Exercise Routine

Daily physical exercise helps children cope better. Exercise reduces stress, produces endorphins that create a sense of well-being, and enhances overall cognitive function, among other benefits. Encourage your child to engage in some form of daily physical exercise, such as walking, running, playing basketball, jumping on a trampoline, dancing, skateboarding, riding a bicycle, playing tennis, etc. Help her find exercises that she enjoys so that she is more likely to stick to doing them. Consider having the whole family do an exercise together.

Establishing a Relaxation Routine

Relaxation exercises are described in the *Panic Attack Strategies* section on p. 96 because they help your child get through anxiety attacks. However, regularly practicing these techniques when calm and in control as a proactive strategy is key. The more children practice, the more easily they are able to use the techniques when they are worried or anxious. Relaxation exercises are like physical exercise—the longer they are practiced, the greater the benefits. Help your child set up a daily relaxation routine that involves practicing visualization, belly breathing, and progressive relaxation as described on pages 100 through 102.

Minimizing Distractions When Studying

Multitasking when doing homework—listening to loud music, watching TV, browsing social media—is a potential anxiety trigger. Distractions like these negatively affect concentration, the retention of information, and how the brain learns. Research shows that when the brain tries to do two things at once, it "divides and conquers," dedicating half of its gray matter to each task, minimizing performance on both. Cognitive performance declines when children pay attention to many media channels at once, and they are likely to make more errors, feel more tired, and then worry excessively that they are not performing at their best. Therefore, teach your child to:

- Reduce noise levels while studying or doing homework. Find a quiet place away from family members who are talking or otherwise making noise. Turn off the TV and turn off or lower the volume of background music. (Soft, calming music without lyrics can help some preteens focus more.)

- Turn off cell phones to avoid being distracted by texts, tweets, and other social media notifications.

- Avoid multitasking. Do not try to play a video game or read funny memes on the Internet while studying.

Planning Activities in Advance

Some children get anxious when they find themselves with a lot of down time. They rely on social media or their parents to keep them occupied when they feel bored or have isolated themselves from others out of fear. These children will benefit by planning activities in advance. Foster creativity in your child and teach him to entertain himself.

- Suggest that he create an "I have nothing to do" storage cabinet that contains a deck of cards, board games, jigsaw puzzles, journals for writing in, drawing paper, and art supplies.
- Encourage him to call a friend and make plans in advance for weekends or other days off from school. Remind him occasionally.

Setting a Bedtime Routine

Ideally, children should have at least eight hours of uninterrupted sleep each night, in their own beds. To reach this goal, help your child set up an evening routine that helps her slowly unwind before bedtime. For example, you might encourage her to:

- Take a warm shower or bath.
- Read a few pages of a book while lying in bed.
- Spend a few minutes talking to you about her day and what she can look forward to the next day.
- Write in a gratitude journal (see next section).

Keeping a Gratitude Journal

Writing about things you are grateful for helps develop a positive attitude, which helps with stress management. Encourage and coach your child to write in a gratitude journal daily and share these tips with him:

- Keep the journal by his bed.
- Commit to writing in it every day on a regular schedule. Writing in it as part of his bedtime routine allows him to go to sleep with positive thoughts from the day.
- Use a paper journal and pen instead of keeping an online journal on the computer, if possible.
- Write only positive things, and write at least three things.
- Write in any format he is most comfortable with—write in paragraphs, make lists, supplement with sketches, etc.
- If struggling to think of something to write, ask himself:
  What was the best part of my day?
  What is something that made me happy?
  What am I grateful for?

Panic Attack Strategies

These strategies can stop panic attacks before they become full-blown or reduce the intensity of panic attacks. When your child feels a panic attack coming on or is in the middle of one, encourage her to try some of these.

Using Distractions

When children feel anxious and are engaging in negative self-talk, distracting themselves from whatever is stressing them is quite helpful. It is a necessary step to refocusing their energy and resetting the brain. Coach your child to use some of these distraction strategies when she feels anxious:

- Move to a quiet corner or turn away from the upsetting situation and quietly count backward from 30 to 1. Repeat until she feels relaxed. (Counting from 1 to 10 as is sometimes suggested is not recommended because counting to 10 is so automatic for a child that she need not think too hard to do it.)
- Leave the room for a few moments to get a change of scenery.
- Give herself a BIG bear hug to help self-soothe.
- Cuddle with a pet. Not only is doing so soothing, but it can lower blood pressure and reduce stress hormones as well.
- Listen to calming music.

- Stretch with her hands joined together over her head. Move side to side. Bend over and touch her toes.

Engaging in Repetitive Movement

Repetitive movement helps children relax and serves as a good distraction from whatever is stressing them. Encourage your child to do some of the following things when he is feeling anxious:

- Rock back and forth in a rocking chair he has previously identified as his "thinking chair."
- Rock in a hammock.
- Swing on a tree swing or swing set.
- Swim laps.
- Roll playdough into balls.
- Throw a ball against a wall.
- Cycle on a stationary bike.
- Shoot a basketball into a basket.
- Jump on a trampoline.
- Rub a piece of material with an interesting texture, like velcro or velvet, that he keeps in his pocket for self-soothing.
- Clap hands in a counterclockwise circle 5 times.
- Tap a repetitive beat with the hands or a pencil.
- Squeeze a stress ball 10 times with each hand.
- Spin a fidget spinner toy.
- Bounce on a rubber yoga ball.

Engaging in Bursts of Exercise

Sometimes getting the heart pounding in short bursts helps reduce anxiety. When your child is feeling overwhelmed with worry, encourage her to do a quick exercise, like running in place for 30 seconds, resting for 60 seconds, and running in place again for 60 seconds. After the exercise ask her to rate her anxiety level from 0 (no fear) to 10 (severe fear). Have her repeat the exercise until her anxiety drops by at least half, preferably until she rates it down to a 3. Try different exercises one at a time until you find one that works best for her.

Challenging Negative Thoughts

Challenging negative self-talk during an anxiety attack can help your child reach his prefrontal cortex and take control of his fight, flight, or freeze reaction. If he can identify what is happening, he might even be able to find humor in it and tell himself, *There goes my "protector brain," at it again!* Coach him to examine his negative thoughts and question himself when he feels anxious. The more often he practices this strategy, the less often "what ifs" will invade his thinking.

- Identify the negative thought. (*What am I thinking that has me upset?*)
- Remind himself he might be experiencing a false alarm. (*Just because I am thinking this, doesn't make it true. My "worry brain" might be taking over and sending me a false alarm.*)

- Challenge the negative thought. (*So…is there an immediate threat I should be worried about, or is this a false alarm? What does the evidence point to?*)
- If the evidence points to a false alarm, deliberately replace the negative thoughts with positive thoughts. (*What can I say to myself instead? What are the positives in this situation?*)

Creating Positivity

Focusing on the positive improves mood and builds resilience to stress. Coach your child to intentionally create positivity when she is feeling anxious. Some things she can do are:

- Use positive self-talk such as, "This is hard for me, but I can do it."
- Think about at least one thing she is thankful for and one thing that is going well in her life.
- Create a positive moment like cuddling with a pet, re-reading something nice someone wrote to her, watching a funny or heart-warming video, or listening to a favorite song.

Relaxing in Your Own Cave

Children like having a special place to go when they feel upset or want to do breathing or relaxation exercises in private. Help your child create his own "cave," an area for alone time. This might be an entire room, a nook in the corner of a room, a large closet, a tree house, or a tent he makes with blankets. Encourage him to make it his own. He might want to decorate it with peaceful pictures, add comfortable throw cushions or blankets, include a tray or table with paper and art supplies handy, or store favorite books there. When he feels anxious, encourage him to go to his cave to relax, listen to soothing music (preferably without lyrics), read a book, write, draw, and so on.

Using Visualization and Guided Imagery

Your child can calm herself during an anxiety attack by taking a few moments to visualize her "happy place"—a place, situation, or activity that she associates with being happy and calm, something safe, secure, and worry-free that brings her a sense of peacefulness and allows her mind to de-stress. She should make every effort to focus on being present in the moment. Her happy place does not have to be real. It can be a bench in her house or school yard, an imagined scenic view of the mountains, or simply a special place that is imprinted in her heart and mind that will allow her mind to be distracted so she can find her inner calm. The first few times she tries this, it will help for you to guide her with your words. Encourage her to imagine as much detail as possible. Tell her to:

- Close her eyes and get in a comfortable position.
- Bring to mind her happy place.
- Imagine what she sees.
- Imagine what she hears.

- Imagine what she tastes, if applicable.
- Imagine what she smells.
- Imagine what sensations she feels on her body.

Doing Belly Breathing Exercises

Belly breathing, also called diaphragm breathing, means using the diaphragm to take slow, deep breaths that move the belly up and down (versus taking fast, shallow breaths that move the chest). When done properly, it can reverse the stress response and help your child to calm down quickly. An anxious child tends to breathe more quickly, which can make him dizzy, lightheaded, and even more anxious. By deliberately slowing down his breath, he can prevent these additional symptoms and even reduce anxiety.

Some preteens find it difficult to focus on their breathing and thus might need the help of a trained therapist to learn how to do breathing exercises, after which they can practice them with you. Once your child learns the method, he should practice regularly, even when he is calm. When he masters deep breathing, he will be able to use it automatically to induce the relaxation response when dealing with stressful situations. Instructions:

- Breathe slowly through the nose to a count of four, filling the belly like a balloon, and then slowly let the air out through the mouth to a count of four, deflating the belly. (Breath with your child, guiding him with your words: "In through your nose...1, 2, 3, 4...out through your mouth...4, 3, 2, 1.")

- Imagine taking in a favorite smell or sound or color with each inhale and sending it slowly throughout the whole body.
- Pay attention only to the feeling of the breath. If the mind wanders, do not give up; simply refocus on the breath.

Doing Progressive Relaxation Exercises

Progressive relaxation exercises involve building up tension in the muscles and then relaxing them. Experiencing the contrast between tension and relaxation in the body helps children better recognize when they are starting to get anxious. Once they are more mindful of the physical signs of anxiety, they can act on it more quickly. While there are many techniques for learning progressive relaxation, the following method progresses from the face down to the feet and is often used for preteens.

To guide your child through this exercise, ask her to lie down on her back with her arms by her sides and to close her eyes. Have her do each of the following actions, hold while counting to five, and then relax for a few seconds while taking a slow deep breath. Repeat two more times before moving on to the next action. Give her the following instructions:

- Tighten the muscles on your forehead.
  Count to five: 1...2...3...4...5.

Relax and take a slow, deep breath: in…and out…
(Repeat two times.)

- Wrinkle your nose like you smell something unpleasant.
  Count to five: 1…2…3…4…5.
  Relax and take a slow, deep breath: in…and out…
  (Repeat two times.)

- Scrunch up your whole face.
  Count to five: 1…2…3…4…5.
  Relax and take a slow, deep breath: in…and out…
  (Repeat two times.)

- Pretend you are chewing something hard.
  Count to five: 1…2…3…4…5.
  Relax and take a slow, deep breath: in…and out…
  (Repeat two times.)

- Tighten your shoulders by pulling them up toward your ears.
  Count to five: 1…2…3…4…5.
  Relax and take a slow, deep breath: in…and out…
  (Repeat two times.)

- Tightly clench your right hand into a fist.
  Count to five: 1…2…3…4…5.
  Relax and take a slow, deep breath: in…and out…
  (Repeat two times.)

- Tightly clench your left hand into a fist.
  Count to five: 1…2…3…4…5.

Relax and take a slow, deep breath: in…and out…
(Repeat two times.)

- Tightly clench both hands into fists at the same time.
Count to five: 1…2…3…4…5.
Relax and take a slow, deep breath: in…and out…
(Repeat two times.)

- Stretch your arms as far above your head as you can.
Count to five: 1…2…3…4…5.
Relax and take a slow, deep breath: in…and out…
(Repeat two times.)

- Tighten and squeeze your stomach as hard as you can.
Count to five: 1…2…3…4…5.
Relax and take a slow, deep breath: in…and out…
(Repeat two times.)

- Squeeze your thighs together tightly.
Count to five: 1…2…3…4…5.
Relax and take a slow, deep breath: in…and out…
(Repeat two times.)

- Squeeze your knees together tightly.
Count to five: 1…2…3…4…5.
Relax and take a slow, deep breath: in…and out…
(Repeat two times.)

- Tense your legs by pulling your toes up toward your head.
Count to five: 1…2…3…4…5.

Relax and take a slow, deep breath: in…and out…
(Repeat two times.)

Using Scent as a Relaxation Tool

Some children are calmed by breathing in pleasant scents, such as lavender. Have your child experiment with scents to discover whether they are an effective tool for her. If so, during breathing or relaxation exercises, homework time, bedtime, or any other time she is intentional about relaxing, she can try some of the following strategies:

- Diffuse essential oils into the room.
- Inhale essential oils; take a few sniffs of the bottles they come in.
- Wear a lightly scented, pleasant fragrance.
- Light a scented candle.
- Apply scented lotion.
- Use scented soaps or bubble baths that do not contain harmful additives such as sulfates, parabens, or silicones.

Communication Strategies

These strategies improve communication in the family. Effective communication is critical for helping your child.

Setting Family Rules Together

When children know what is expected of them at home, and especially when they have some say in those expectations, they experience less anxiety. Have a family meeting and together set rules and expectations. Give each family member the opportunity to provide input and use it to set fair rules when reasonable and appropriate. Try to establish a routine that works for everyone. Some of the goals of the family meeting might be to:

- Specify bedtimes, chores, and responsibilities around the house.
- Establish homework routines.
- Limit the amount of time spent on TV, video games, and the computer.
- Determine where mobile devices are kept during homework time.

Practicing Communicating Feelings

Stress to your child the importance of communicating and expressing her feelings with words. Encourage him to try to label the feelings he experiences throughout the day. Model the use of such vocabulary; for example, "It looks like you're happy today."

Using "I Statements"

When children (and adults!) feel upset by someone, they tend to use "you statements," such as, "You shouldn't have done that. You're so mean!" These types of statements are judgmental and confrontational and thus usually cause the offender to react defensively. A more effective approach is to use "I statements"—statements that explain how the other person's behavior made you feel and what you would like the other person to do instead. Examples of "I statements":

- I don't like it when you cut in front of me without asking. Please don't do it again.
- When you tease me in front of your friends, I feel very embarrassed. Please don't do it again.
- I feel hurt when you ignore me. Please try to acknowledge me when I'm talking to you, even if it is to say you'd rather not talk right now or you're busy.
- I don't like it when you take things from my desk without asking. Please ask me next time.

Not Avoiding Difficult Conversations

Parents and caregivers do not want to cause anxiety and distress in their children, understandably. This often results in avoiding difficult conversations. However, an important part of your child's success in working through his anxiety is having non-threatening conversations about what is bothering him. Do not shy away from opportunities to talk to your child about his anxiety or difficult things going on in his life. Keep these things in mind:

- Your child probably will not walk up to you and say, "I'm anxious. Let's talk." You must pay attention to his self-talk. Listen for words that signal he is feeling anxious, like "worried," "confused," "annoyed," "angry," etc. Pay attention to body language that communicates anxiety, such as clenched fists, rapid breathing, or tears.

- Avoid lashing out at your child while he is upset and acting out. Wait until he is calm to validate his feelings, tell him it is not okay to act the way he did, and ask him to brainstorm what he could have done or said instead.

- Let your child's interests, questions, and thoughts guide the depth of the conversation. When he is ready to express more thoughts or has more questions, he will come back to you.

Listening Closely

Some children will want to talk about difficult situations they are worrying about, and some will not. Both reactions are common and natural. Either way, it is important to give them the opportunity to share their thoughts, feelings, and questions comfortably, without you becoming overly emotional or punitive. If your child does not feel like talking, do not force the discussion. Check in periodically and let her know you are ready to listen whenever she wants to talk. Remember to:

- Actively listen to her concerns.
- Attend to her body language, which might give you some insight into her mood.
- Validate her emotions. If she is afraid, never belittle the fear as a way of forcing her to overcome it. Avoid saying things that minimize her distress; for example, do not say, "Don't be ridiculous," "That's silly," or "You're not going to die because you worry a lot." No matter how unreasonable your child's fear seems to you, to her the fear is very real.
- Encourage respectful conversation and discussion in a calm manner.
- Use words of encouragement that focus on the process, like studying and learning, rather than the end result, like grades. For example:

"Good for you, I can see you worked hard on this."

"Great thinking! You should be proud of yourself."

"You must be practicing. Keep up the hard work."

"Keep it up!"

"Way to go! I'm proud of you."

"Nothing can stop you now. Your hard work is paying off."

Strategy Log

As you explore and practice the brain-smart strategies from this book in your daily lives, log the results on the following pages. Take notes on what was helpful for your child, what was not helpful, and what you might want to do differently next time. Use the logs as a quick reference every time you want to practice a strategy.

Note: This book contains six log pages. Making copies of a blank log page is recommended so that you can take notes on more than six strategies.

Strategy name: _____

Describe how and in what situation you used the strategy.

_____

_____

_____

_____

Was it helpful? _____

What were the challenges?

_____

_____

_____

_____

What will you do differently next time you try it?

_____

_____

_____

_____

_____

_____

Strategy name: _____

Describe how and in what situation you used the strategy.

_____

_____

_____

_____

Was it helpful? _____

What were the challenges?

_____

_____

_____

_____

What will you do differently next time you try it?

_____

_____

_____

_____

_____

Strategy name: _____

Describe how and in what situation you used the strategy.

_____

_____

_____

_____

Was it helpful? _____

What were the challenges?

_____

_____

_____

_____

What will you do differently next time you try it?

_____

_____

_____

_____

_____

Strategy name: _____

Describe how and in what situation you used the strategy.

_____

_____

_____

_____

Was it helpful? _____

What were the challenges?

_____

_____

_____

_____

What will you do differently next time you try it?

_____

_____

_____

_____

_____

Strategy name: _____

Describe how and in what situation you used the strategy.

_____

_____

_____

_____

Was it helpful? _____

What were the challenges?

_____

_____

_____

_____

What will you do differently next time you try it?

_____

_____

_____

_____

_____

Strategy name: _____

Describe how and in what situation you used the strategy.

_____

_____

_____

_____

Was it helpful? _____

What were the challenges?

_____

_____

_____

_____

What will you do differently next time you try it?

_____

_____

_____

_____

_____

_____

Additional Resources for Parents and Preteens

Books

Chansky, Tamar E. *Freeing Your Child: from Negative Thinking*. Da Capo Lifelong, 2008.

Chansky, Tamar E., and Phillip Stern. *Freeing Your Child from Anxiety: Powerful, Practical Solutions to Overcome Your Child's Fears, Phobias, and Worries*. Broadway Books, 2004.

Crist, James J. *What to Do When You're Scared & Worried: A Guide for Kids*. Free Spirit Publishing, 2008.

Eisen, Andrew R., and Linda B. Engler. *Helping Your Child Overcome Separation Anxiety or School Refusal: A Step-by-Step Guide for Parents*. New Harbinger Publications, 2006.

Greene, Ross W. *The Explosive Child*. Harper Collins, 1998.

Huebner, Dawn, and Kara McHale. *Outsmarting Worry: An Older Kid's Guide to Managing Anxiety*. Jessica Kingsley Publishers, 2017.

Huebner, Dawn. *What to Do When You Worry Too Much: A Kid's Guide to Overcoming Anxiety*. Magination Press, 2005.

Pittman, Catherine M., and Elizabeth Karle. *Rewire your Anxious Brain: How to Use the Neuroscience of Fear to End Anxiety, Panic, and Worry*. New Harbinger Publications, 2015.

Thomas, Alex, and Jeff Grimes. *Best Practices in School Psychology V*. National Association of School Psychologists, 2008, pp.1473-1486.

Wilson, Reid, and Lynn Lyons. *Playing with Anxiety: Casey's Guide for Teens & Kids*, 1st ed., BookBaby, 2013.

Websites

adaa.org - Anxiety and Depression Association of America

catnew.dcsdev.org - Coping Cat Parents, Child Anxiety Tales: An Online Program for Parents to Learn Managing Child Stress and Anxiety

childanxiety.net - The Child Anxiety Network

gozen.com/allprograms/ - GoZen! Anxiety/Stress Relief Program

worrywisekids.org - Worry Wise Kids

References

"Anxiety Disorders." *National Institute of Mental Health*, U.S. Department of Health and Human Services, www.nimh.nih.gov//health/topics/anxiety-disorders/index.shtml.

Bitsko Rebecca H, et al. "Epidemiology and Impact of Health Care Provider-Diagnosed Anxiety and Depression Among US Children." *Journal of Developmental and Behavioral Pediatrics: JDBP*, U.S. National Library of Medicine, pubmed.ncbi.nlm.nih.gov/29688990/. Published online before print April 24, 2018.

Chansky, Tamar E. *Freeing Your Child from Anxiety: Practical Strategies to Overcome Fears, Worries, and Phobias and Be Prepared for Life–from Toddlers to Teens*. Harmony, 2014.

Diagnostic and Statistical Manual of Mental Disorders, Fifth Edition (DSM-5®). American Psychiatric Publishing, 2013.

Forster, Gina L., et al. "The Role of the Amygdala in Anxiety Disorders." *IntechOpen*, 19 Dec. 2012, www.intechopen.com/books/the-amygdala-a-discrete-multitasking-manager/the-role-of-the-amygdala-in-anxiety-disorders, doi: 10.5772/50323.

Ghandour, Reem M., et al. "Prevalence and Treatment of Depression, Anxiety, and Conduct Problems in US Children." *The Journal of Pediatrics*, Mosby, 12 Oct. 2018, www.sciencedirect.com/science/article/pii/S0022347618312 927. Published online before print October 12, 2018.

Huberty, Thomas J. "Anxiety & Anxiety Disorders in Children: Information for Parents." *National Association of School Psychologists (NASP)*, www.nasponline.org/resources-and-publications/resources-and-podcasts/mental-health/mental-health-disorders/anxiety-and-anxiety-disorders-in-children-information-for-parents.

National Comorbidity Survey, www.hcp.med.harvard.edu/ncs/index.php. Accessed August 2017.

"The State of Mental Health in America." *Mental Health America*, www.mhanational.org/issues/state-mental-health-america. Accessed 2020.

"Stress in America™ 2020: A National Mental Health Crisis." *American Psychological Association*, American Psychological Association, www.apa.org/news/press/releases/stress/2020/report-october.

Wilson, Robert R., and Lynn Lyons. *Anxious Kids, Anxious Parents: 7 Ways to Stop the Worry Cycle and Raise Courageous & Independent Children.* Health Communications, Inc., 2013.

About the Author

Patricia Pantelias Gage, PhD
School Psychologist

Patricia Pantelias Gage, PhD has been a practicing school psychologist for more than 30 years. She holds a Bachelor of Arts degree in Elementary Education and Psychology from Hunter College, a master's degree in School Psychological Services, and a PhD in Child/School Psychology from New York University. She has been an active member of her community as a compassionate advocate for children's social and emotional wellness and the rights of students with learning differences. She has been instrumental in implementing several successful programs in Florida, such as the Mainstream Instructional and Behavioral Consultation Program for the Martin County Schools; the Weebiscus preschool program for Hibiscus Children Center, a shelter for abused and neglected children; and the Academic Center at The Pine School.

Dr. Gage has served on the Board of the Rotary Club of Stuart, The Pine School, and Hibiscus Children Center. She was a tireless member of The Rotary Foundation/ Matching Grants, the Rotary Youth Leadership Assembly, and the District 6930 Literacy Committee. She was the mental health counselor for the district 6930 Rotary Student Exchange Program and the

Rotary Youth Leadership Assembly. She was a member of the Advisory Board of the Martin Memorial Foundation and a founder of the Women in Philanthropy group. Dr. Gage is a proud co-founder of a second company, Hang In There, LLC, which produces a series of parenting guides and has donated over 15,000 guides and books to local organizations serving children and new parents. Both the guides and Dr. Gage's book *Long Live the Queen: Help for Children Who Have a Loved One with Cancer* are Mom's Choice Award Gold recipients. Dr. Gage also is the co-author of *Mrs. Feathergreen Might Be a Superhero* and *Coach Your Teen to Get Organized and Learn: A Parent Guide.*

Dr. Gage was the 2003 Martin County recipient of the Soroptimist International Women of Distinction award and was selected Rotarian of the Year 2002-2003 and 2009-2010. She is a member of the National Association of School Psychologists and the American Psychological Association.

She is married to Dr. Joseph Gage, a local Cardiologist, and is the proud mother of two wonderful sons. She loves photography, cooking, gardening, and traveling with her family. Dr. Gage's "happy place" is the beach that was just down the street from her childhood home in East Marion, New York. The following photos show what she envisions when she practices visualization and slow, deep breathing to maintain inner peace.

Visualize your own
happy place!

Made in the USA
Columbia, SC
17 May 2022